Seal the Deal: Mastering Sales Objections to Close Every Sale

1. The Objection Overcomer: Closing Deals with Confidence
2. Mastering Objections: The Key to Closing Every Sale
3. From Objections to Agreements: How to Close More Deals
4. Seal the Deal: Conquering Sales Objections Like a Pro
5. Turning No into Yes: The Ultimate Guide to Closing Sales
6. Closing Power: Overcoming Sales Objections for Guaranteed Success
7. Deal Makers: Mastering Objections to Achieve Sales Excellence
8. The Art of Persuasion: Closing Sales by Overcoming Objections
9. Objection Mastery: Proven Strategies to Close Any Sale
10. Yes, You Can! Overcoming Objections and Closing Deals

Unlock your full sales potential with Seal the Deal: Mastering Sales Objections to Close Every Sale. This essential guide is your blueprint to becoming a sales powerhouse, turning objections into opportunities and closing every deal with confidence.

In this game-changing book, you'll dive deep into ten powerful chapters, each packed with actionable strategies to help you master the art of overcoming objections. Start with "The Objection Overcomer: Closing Deals with Confidence," where you'll learn to handle objections with poise and turn them into closing opportunities. Explore "Mastering Objections: The Key to Closing Every Sale," which reveals the secrets to navigating tough objections with ease.

Whether you're a seasoned professional or new to sales, Seal the Deal will elevate your skills. Discover how to transform "No" into "Yes" with "Turning No into Yes: The Ultimate Guide to Closing Sales," and cement your success with "Objection Mastery: Proven Strategies to Close Any Sale."

By the time you finish, you'll have a complete toolkit for closing deals, every time. Say goodbye to lost opportunities and hello to a world where objections are just stepping stones to success. Don't just sell—seal the deal! Get your copy today and start mastering objections like a pro.

The Objection Overcomer: Closing Deals with Confidence

Sales objections are an inevitable part of the sales process, but they should not be seen as insurmountable hurdles. Instead, objections can provide valuable opportunities to address concerns, clarify misunderstandings, and ultimately strengthen the relationship with potential clients. Mastering the art of overcoming sales objections is crucial for any salesperson aiming to close deals with confidence. This report delves into the nature of sales objections, strategies to effectively address them, and real-world examples to illustrate how to turn objections into successful sales.

Understanding Sales Objections

The Nature of Sales Objections

Sales objections typically arise when a potential buyer expresses concerns or hesitations about a product or service. These objections can stem from various sources, such as perceived risks, budget constraints, lack of trust, or simply a need for more information. It is essential to understand that objections are not outright rejections but rather expressions of interest that need further exploration and resolution.

Common Types of Objections

1. Price Objections: Concerns about the cost of the product or service.
2. Value Objections: Doubts about the product's benefits relative to its cost.

3. Timing Objections: Hesitations due to perceived bad timing or other priorities.
4. Need Objections: Uncertainty about whether the product meets their needs.
5. Trust Objections: Lack of trust in the company, product, or salesperson.

Strategies for Overcoming Sales Objections

Active Listening

Active listening involves fully concentrating, understanding, responding, and remembering what the client is saying. By actively listening to the objections, a salesperson can gain insights into the client's concerns and address them more effectively.

Example:
A potential client expresses concern about the price of a software subscription. By listening actively, the salesperson learns that the client is worried about the cost relative to their budget for the quarter. The salesperson can then address this specific concern by offering a payment plan or highlighting cost-saving features of the software.

Empathy and Understanding

Empathy is crucial in overcoming objections. Demonstrating understanding and empathy helps build rapport and trust with the client. Acknowledge their concerns and show that you are genuinely interested in finding a solution that works for them.

Example:

If a client is hesitant about switching to a new service provider due to past negative experiences, showing empathy and sharing stories of other clients who successfully made the switch can help alleviate their concerns.

Clarifying and Validating

Clarification involves asking questions to fully understand the objection, while validation reassures the client that their concerns are legitimate. This approach not only addresses the specific objection but also reinforces the salesperson's credibility.

Example:
A client expresses uncertainty about the compatibility of a new software with their existing systems. The salesperson can clarify by asking

detailed questions about the client's current setup and validate their concern by providing case studies or testimonials from other clients with similar systems.

Providing Evidence and Examples

Concrete evidence and examples, such as case studies, testimonials, and demonstrations, can effectively counter objections. Providing proof of past successes and demonstrating the product's benefits can alleviate doubts and build confidence.

Example:
When a client questions the ROI of a marketing service, the salesperson can present case studies showing significant ROI achieved by similar businesses. Additionally, offering a demonstration or trial period can

provide firsthand experience of the benefits.

Reframing the Objection

Reframing involves turning the objection into a positive aspect or showing a different perspective. This technique helps clients see the situation in a new light and can diminish their concerns.

Example:
If a client objects to the initial cost of a high-quality product, the salesperson can reframe this by emphasizing the long-term savings and superior performance, which ultimately offers better value compared to cheaper alternatives.

Offering Alternatives and Solutions

Flexibility in offering alternatives or customized solutions can address objections effectively. This approach shows that the salesperson is willing to work with the client to find a mutually beneficial solution.

Example:
A client is concerned about the implementation timeline of a new service. The salesperson can offer alternative solutions, such as phased implementation or additional support, to accommodate the client's schedule and alleviate their concerns.

Practical Applications and Real-World Examples

Example 1: Overcoming Price Objections

Scenario: A small business owner is hesitant to invest in a new CRM system due to its high cost.

Approach:
- Active Listening: The salesperson listens to the client's budget concerns and asks questions to understand their financial constraints.
- Providing Evidence: The salesperson presents data showing how the CRM system has helped similar businesses increase revenue and reduce operational costs.
- Reframing the Objection: The salesperson highlights the long-term cost savings and improved efficiency that will outweigh the initial investment.

Outcome: The client, reassured by the evidence and reframing, agrees to a flexible payment plan, leading to a successful sale.

Example 2: Addressing Timing Objections

Scenario: A potential client is interested in a new project management tool but feels it's not the right time to switch due to ongoing projects.

Approach:
- Empathy and Understanding: The salesperson acknowledges the client's concern about the timing and expresses understanding.
- Clarifying and Validating: The salesperson asks detailed questions about the client's current projects and timeline.
- Offering Alternatives: The salesperson suggests a phased implementation plan that aligns with

the client's schedule and minimizes disruption.

Outcome: The client appreciates the tailored solution and agrees to start the implementation process after completing the current projects.

Example 3: Handling Trust Objections

Scenario: A client is wary of switching to a new supplier due to a negative experience with a previous supplier.

Approach:
- Empathy and Understanding: The salesperson empathizes with the client's past experiences and acknowledges their hesitation.
- Providing Evidence: The salesperson shares testimonials from satisfied

customers and offers a trial period to build trust.
- Reframing the Objection: The salesperson reframes the situation by emphasizing the superior customer service and support provided by their company.

Outcome: The client, reassured by the evidence and the trial period, decides to give the new supplier a chance, leading to a successful partnership.

Conclusion

Overcoming sales objections is an art that requires active listening, empathy, understanding, and strategic problem-solving. By employing these techniques, salespeople can turn objections into opportunities, build stronger relationships with clients, and close deals with confidence. Mastering the art of handling objections not only enhances sales performance but also contributes to long-term customer satisfaction and loyalty. The strategies and real-world examples discussed in this report provide a roadmap for sales professionals aiming to become adept at overcoming objections and achieving sales success. Embrace these techniques, and watch your ability to close deals and build lasting client relationships flourish.

Mastering Objections: The Key to Closing Every Sale

Sales objections are an inherent part of the sales process, presenting both challenges and opportunities. The ability to master objections is a crucial skill for any salesperson aiming to close deals and build lasting customer relationships. This report explores the nature of sales objections, effective strategies for overcoming them, and real-world examples that illustrate the transformative power of mastering objections.

Understanding Sales Objections

The Nature of Sales Objections

Sales objections occur when a prospective customer expresses concerns, doubts, or resistance regarding a product or service. These objections can be seen as hurdles that need to be addressed for a successful sale. However, objections are not outright rejections; they often indicate interest and the need for further information or reassurance.

Common Types of Sales Objections

1. Price Objections: Concerns about the cost of the product or service.
2. Value Objections: Doubts about the benefits of the product relative to its cost.
3. Timing Objections: Hesitations due to perceived bad timing or other priorities.
4. Need Objections: Uncertainty about whether the product meets the prospect's needs.
5. Trust Objections: Lack of trust in the company, product, or salesperson.

Strategies for Overcoming Sales Objections

Active Listening

Active listening involves fully concentrating, understanding, responding, and remembering what the prospect is saying. By actively listening, salespeople can better understand the underlying concerns and address them effectively.

Example:
A prospect is concerned about the price of a software solution. By listening attentively, the salesperson learns that the prospect is worried about fitting the purchase into their current budget. The salesperson can then address this specific concern by offering a payment plan or highlighting cost-saving features of the software.

Empathy and Understanding

Demonstrating empathy and understanding helps build rapport and trust with the prospect. Acknowledging their concerns shows that the salesperson is genuinely interested in finding a solution that works for them.

Example:
If a prospect is hesitant about switching to a new service provider due to past negative experiences, showing empathy and sharing success stories of other clients who made the switch can help alleviate their concerns.

Clarifying and Validating

Clarification involves asking questions to fully understand the objection, while validation reassures the prospect that their concerns are legitimate. This approach not only addresses the specific objection but also reinforces the salesperson's credibility.

Example:
A prospect expresses uncertainty about the compatibility of a new software with their existing systems. The salesperson can clarify by asking detailed questions about the prospect's current setup and validate their concern by providing case studies or testimonials from other clients with similar systems.

Providing Evidence and Examples

Concrete evidence and examples, such as case studies, testimonials, and demonstrations, can effectively counter objections. Providing proof of past successes and demonstrating the product's benefits can alleviate doubts and build confidence.

Example:
When a prospect questions the ROI of a marketing service, the

salesperson can present case studies showing significant ROI achieved by similar businesses. Additionally, offering a demonstration or trial period can provide firsthand experience of the benefits.

Reframing the Objection

Reframing involves turning the objection into a positive aspect or showing a different perspective. This technique helps prospects see the situation in a new light and can diminish their concerns.

Example:
If a prospect objects to the initial cost of a high-quality product, the salesperson can reframe this by emphasizing the long-term savings and superior performance, which ultimately offers better value compared to cheaper alternatives.

Offering Alternatives and Solutions

Flexibility in offering alternatives or customized solutions can address objections effectively. This approach shows that the salesperson is willing to work with the prospect to find a mutually beneficial solution.

Example:
A prospect is concerned about the implementation timeline of a new service. The salesperson can offer alternative solutions, such as phased implementation or additional support, to accommodate the prospect's schedule and alleviate their concerns.

Practical Applications and Real-World Examples

Example 1: Overcoming Price Objections

Scenario: A small business owner is hesitant to invest in a new CRM system due to its high cost.

Approach:
- Active Listening: The salesperson listens to the client's budget concerns and asks questions to understand their financial constraints.
- Providing Evidence: The salesperson presents data showing how the CRM system has helped similar businesses increase revenue and reduce operational costs.
- Reframing the Objection: The salesperson highlights the long-term cost savings and improved efficiency that will outweigh the initial investment.

Outcome: The client, reassured by the evidence and reframing, agrees to a flexible payment plan, leading to a successful sale.

Example 2: Addressing Timing Objections

Scenario: A potential client is interested in a new project management tool but feels it's not the right time to switch due to ongoing projects.

Approach:
- Empathy and Understanding: The salesperson acknowledges the client's concern about the timing and expresses understanding.
- Clarifying and Validating: The salesperson asks detailed questions about the client's current projects and timeline.

- Offering Alternatives: The salesperson suggests a phased implementation plan that aligns with the client's schedule and minimizes disruption.

Outcome: The client appreciates the tailored solution and agrees to start the implementation process after completing the current projects.

Example 3: Handling Trust Objections

Scenario: A client is wary of switching to a new supplier due to a negative experience with a previous supplier.

Approach:
- Empathy and Understanding: The salesperson empathizes with the client's past experiences and acknowledges their hesitation.

- Providing Evidence: The salesperson shares testimonials from satisfied customers and offers a trial period to build trust.
- Reframing the Objection: The salesperson reframes the situation by emphasizing the superior customer service and support provided by their company.

Outcome: The client, reassured by the evidence and the trial period, decides to give the new supplier a chance, leading to a successful partnership.

Advanced Techniques for Overcoming Objections

The Feel, Felt, Found Method

This method involves empathizing with the prospect's feelings, sharing a story of someone who felt the same way, and explaining what they found after using the product.

 Example:
Scenario: A prospect is hesitant about the complexity of a new software system.

Approach:
- Feel: "I understand how you feel. Many of our clients initially felt the same way about the complexity."
- Felt: "One of our clients, a mid-sized company, felt overwhelmed at first."
- Found: "But they found that with our comprehensive training and support, they were able to master the software quickly and saw significant improvements in their productivity."

Outcome: The prospect feels reassured by the shared experience and is more willing to proceed with the purchase.

The Socratic Method

The Socratic Method involves asking a series of questions to help the prospect come to their own conclusion about the benefits of the product.

Example:
Scenario: A prospect is unsure about the necessity of a new marketing service.

Approach:
- Question: "What are your current marketing goals?"
- Follow-up Question: "What challenges are you facing in achieving those goals?"
- Next Question: "How do you think a targeted marketing service could help overcome those challenges?"

Outcome: Through a series of guided questions, the prospect recognizes the value of the marketing service and how it can help achieve their goals.

Psychological Techniques in Overcoming Objections

Building Rapport

Building rapport with the prospect helps establish trust and makes them more receptive to your solutions. This involves finding common ground, showing genuine interest, and maintaining a positive and friendly demeanor.

Example:
A salesperson finds out that a prospect enjoys the same sport. By discussing their shared interest, the salesperson builds a connection that

makes the prospect more open to hearing about the product.

Using Social Proof

People tend to follow the actions of others, especially in uncertain situations. Sharing testimonials, case studies, and success stories can leverage social proof to overcome objections.

Example:
A prospect is unsure about the effectiveness of a new service. The salesperson shares testimonials and case studies from similar clients who experienced positive results, providing reassurance and increasing the prospect's confidence in the product.

Creating a Sense of Urgency

Creating a sense of urgency can prompt the prospect to take action by emphasizing limited-time offers or highlighting the immediate benefits of the product.

Example:
A salesperson informs the prospect of a limited-time discount or a promotional offer that adds extra value to the purchase, encouraging the prospect to make a decision sooner rather than later.

Conclusion

Mastering objections is a critical skill that can significantly enhance a salesperson's ability to close deals and build long-term customer relationships. By employing strategies such as active listening, empathy, clarifying and validating concerns, providing evidence, reframing objections, and offering alternatives, salespeople can effectively address and overcome objections. Advanced techniques like the Feel, Felt, Found method and the Socratic Method, along with psychological approaches like building rapport, using social proof, and creating urgency, further empower sales professionals to navigate objections successfully.

Through real-world examples and practical applications, this report demonstrates that objections are not barriers but opportunities to engage with prospects, understand their needs, and provide tailored solutions. By mastering the art of overcoming objections, salespeople can turn challenges into triumphs, closing more deals and achieving sustained success in their sales careers. Embrace these strategies, refine your approach, and watch your sales performance soar as you transform objections into opportunities for growth and success.

From Objections to Agreements: How to Close More Deals

Sales objections are a natural part of the sales process. They can arise from various factors, such as price, value, timing, need, or trust. However, objections should not be seen as barriers but rather as opportunities to understand the prospect's concerns and work towards an agreement. This report explores the nature of sales objections, effective strategies to address them, and real-world examples to demonstrate how turning objections into agreements can significantly enhance sales success.

Understanding Sales Objections

The Nature of Sales Objections

Sales objections occur when a potential customer expresses hesitation or reluctance to proceed with a purchase. These objections are not outright rejections but rather indications of the prospect's need for more information, reassurance, or a different perspective. Understanding the underlying reasons for objections is crucial in addressing them effectively.

Common Types of Sales Objections

1. Price Objections: Concerns about the cost of the product or service.

2. Value Objections: Doubts about the benefits or value of the product relative to its cost.
3. Timing Objections: Hesitations due to perceived bad timing or other priorities.
4. Need Objections: Uncertainty about whether the product meets the prospect's needs.
5. Trust Objections: Lack of trust in the company, product, or salesperson.

Strategies for Turning Objections into Agreements

Active Listening

Active listening involves fully concentrating on what the prospect is saying, understanding their concerns, responding thoughtfully, and remembering the details. This approach helps in accurately identifying the root of the objection and addressing it effectively.

Example:
A prospect expresses concern about the high cost of a new software solution. By actively listening, the salesperson learns that the prospect is worried about fitting the purchase into their budget. The salesperson can then address this specific concern by offering a payment plan or highlighting cost-saving features of the software.

Empathy and Understanding

Demonstrating empathy and understanding helps build rapport and trust with the prospect. Acknowledging their concerns shows that the salesperson is genuinely interested in finding a solution that works for them.

Example:
If a prospect is hesitant about switching to a new service provider due to past negative experiences, showing empathy and sharing success stories of other clients who made the switch can help alleviate their concerns.

Clarifying and Validating

Clarification involves asking questions to fully understand the objection, while validation reassures the prospect that their concerns are legitimate. This approach not only addresses the specific objection but also reinforces the salesperson's credibility.

Example:
A prospect expresses uncertainty about the compatibility of a new

software with their existing systems. The salesperson can clarify by asking detailed questions about the prospect's current setup and validate their concern by providing case studies or testimonials from other clients with similar systems.

Providing Evidence and Examples

Concrete evidence and examples, such as case studies, testimonials, and demonstrations, can effectively counter objections. Providing proof of past successes and demonstrating the product's benefits can alleviate doubts and build confidence.

Example:
When a prospect questions the ROI of a marketing service, the salesperson can present case studies showing significant ROI achieved by similar businesses. Additionally,

offering a demonstration or trial period can provide firsthand experience of the benefits.

Reframing the Objection

Reframing involves turning the objection into a positive aspect or showing a different perspective. This technique helps prospects see the situation in a new light and can diminish their concerns.

Example:
If a prospect objects to the initial cost of a high-quality product, the salesperson can reframe this by emphasizing the long-term savings and superior performance, which ultimately offers better value compared to cheaper alternatives.

Offering Alternatives and Solutions

Flexibility in offering alternatives or customized solutions can address objections effectively. This approach shows that the salesperson is willing to work with the prospect to find a mutually beneficial solution.

Example:
A prospect is concerned about the implementation timeline of a new service. The salesperson can offer alternative solutions, such as phased implementation or additional support, to accommodate the prospect's schedule and alleviate their concerns.

Practical Applications and Real-World Examples

Example 1: Overcoming Price Objections

Scenario: A small business owner is hesitant to invest in a new CRM system due to its high cost.

Approach:
- Active Listening: The salesperson listens to the client's budget concerns and asks questions to understand their financial constraints.
- Providing Evidence: The salesperson presents data showing how the CRM system has helped similar businesses increase revenue and reduce operational costs.
- Reframing the Objection: The salesperson highlights the long-term cost savings and improved efficiency that will outweigh the initial investment.

Outcome: The client, reassured by the evidence and reframing, agrees to a flexible payment plan, leading to a successful sale.

Example 2: Addressing Timing Objections

Scenario: A potential client is interested in a new project management tool but feels it's not the right time to switch due to ongoing projects.

Approach:
- Empathy and Understanding: The salesperson acknowledges the client's concern about the timing and expresses understanding.
- Clarifying and Validating: The salesperson asks detailed questions about the client's current projects and timeline.
- Offering Alternatives: The salesperson suggests a phased implementation plan that aligns with

the client's schedule and minimizes disruption.

Outcome: The client appreciates the tailored solution and agrees to start the implementation process after completing the current projects.

Example 3: Handling Trust Objections

Scenario: A client is wary of switching to a new supplier due to a negative experience with a previous supplier.

Approach:
- Empathy and Understanding: The salesperson empathizes with the client's past experiences and acknowledges their hesitation.
- Providing Evidence: The salesperson shares testimonials from satisfied

customers and offers a trial period to build trust.
- Reframing the Objection: The salesperson reframes the situation by emphasizing the superior customer service and support provided by their company.

Outcome: The client, reassured by the evidence and the trial period, decides to give the new supplier a chance, leading to a successful partnership.

Advanced Techniques for Overcoming Objections

The Feel, Felt, Found Method

This method involves empathizing with the prospect's feelings, sharing a story of someone who felt the same way, and explaining what they found after using the product.

Example:
Scenario: A prospect is hesitant about the complexity of a new software system.

Approach:
- Feel: "I understand how you feel. Many of our clients initially felt the same way about the complexity."
- Felt: "One of our clients, a mid-sized company, felt overwhelmed at first."
- Found: "But they found that with our comprehensive training and support, they were able to master the software quickly and saw significant improvements in their productivity."

Outcome: The prospect feels reassured by the shared experience and is more willing to proceed with the purchase.

The Socratic Method

The Socratic Method involves asking a series of questions to help the prospect come to their own conclusion about the benefits of the product.

Example:
Scenario: A prospect is unsure about the necessity of a new marketing service.

Approach:
- Question: "What are your current marketing goals?"
- Follow-up Question: "What challenges are you facing in achieving those goals?"
- Next Question: "How do you think a targeted marketing service could help overcome those challenges?"

Outcome: Through a series of guided questions, the prospect recognizes the value of the marketing service and how it can help achieve their goals.

Psychological Techniques in Overcoming Objections

Building Rapport

Building rapport with the prospect helps establish trust and makes them more receptive to your solutions. This involves finding common ground, showing genuine interest, and maintaining a positive and friendly demeanor.

Example:
A salesperson finds out that a prospect enjoys the same sport. By discussing their shared interest, the salesperson builds a connection that makes the prospect more open to hearing about the product.

Using Social Proof

People tend to follow the actions of others, especially in uncertain situations. Sharing testimonials, case studies, and success stories can leverage social proof to overcome objections.

Example:
A prospect is unsure about the effectiveness of a new service. The salesperson shares testimonials and case studies from similar clients who experienced positive results, providing reassurance and increasing the prospect's confidence in the product.

Creating a Sense of Urgency

Creating a sense of urgency can prompt the prospect to take action by emphasizing limited-time offers or highlighting the immediate benefits of the product.

Example:
A salesperson informs the prospect of a limited-time discount or a promotional offer that adds extra value to the purchase, encouraging the prospect to make a decision sooner rather than later.

Conclusion

Mastering objections is a critical skill that can significantly enhance a salesperson's ability to close deals and build long-term customer relationships. By employing strategies such as active listening, empathy, clarifying and validating concerns, providing evidence, reframing objections, and offering alternatives, salespeople can effectively address and overcome objections. Advanced techniques like the Feel, Felt, Found method and the Socratic Method, along with psychological approaches like building rapport, using social proof, and creating urgency, further empower sales professionals to navigate objections successfully.

Through real-world examples and practical applications, this report demonstrates that objections are not barriers but opportunities to engage with prospects, understand their needs, and provide tailored solutions. By mastering the art of overcoming objections, salespeople can turn challenges into triumphs, closing more deals and achieving sustained success in their sales careers. Embrace these strategies, refine your approach, and watch your sales performance soar as you transform objections into opportunities for growth and success.

Seal the Deal: Conquering Sales Objections Like a Pro

In the dynamic world of sales, closing deals is both an art and a science. The ability to conquer sales objections effectively distinguishes top performers from the rest. Sales objections, when handled skillfully, can become stepping stones to closing a sale rather than barriers. This report explores top sales closing techniques, the nature of sales objections, and effective strategies to overcome them, supported by real-world examples that illustrate how to turn objections into agreements.

Understanding Sales Objections

The Nature of Sales Objections

Sales objections occur when potential customers express concerns or hesitations about a product or service. These objections are not outright rejections but rather indicators that the prospect needs more information, reassurance, or a different perspective. Objections can stem from various factors, such as price, value, timing, need, or trust.

Common Types of Sales Objections

1. Price Objections: Concerns about the cost of the product or service.
2. Value Objections: Doubts about the benefits or value of the product relative to its cost.
3. Timing Objections: Hesitations due to perceived bad timing or other priorities.

4. Need Objections: Uncertainty about whether the product meets the prospect's needs.
5. Trust Objections: Lack of trust in the company, product, or salesperson.

Top Sales Closing Techniques

1. The Assumptive Close

The assumptive close involves acting as if the prospect has already decided to purchase. This approach relies on the power of suggestion and can be effective in moving the conversation towards closing.

Example:
Scenario: A salesperson selling a software subscription might say, "When would you like to schedule your onboarding session?" instead of "Are you ready to buy?"

2. The Summary Close

The summary close involves summarizing the key benefits and features of the product or service before asking for the sale. This technique helps reinforce the value proposition and address any lingering doubts.

Example:
Scenario: "So, to summarize, our software will help streamline your operations, reduce costs, and improve productivity. Shall we go ahead and get you started with a subscription today?"

3. The Urgency Close

Creating a sense of urgency can prompt the prospect to take immediate action. This can be achieved by emphasizing limited-time offers, exclusive deals, or the immediate benefits of the product.

Example:
Scenario: "We have a special promotion that ends this week, offering a 20% discount on your first year. Would you like to take advantage of this offer?"

4. The Alternative Choice Close

The alternative choice close presents the prospect with two options, both of which lead to a sale. This technique gives the prospect a sense of control while guiding them towards a decision.

Example:
Scenario: "Would you prefer the standard package or the premium package with additional features?"

5. The Question Close

The question close involves asking questions that lead the prospect to acknowledge the benefits of the product and move closer to a decision. This technique encourages engagement and helps uncover any remaining objections.

Example:
Scenario: "How do you see our product fitting into your current operations and helping you achieve your goals?"

6. The Sharp Angle Close

The sharp angle close involves addressing a prospect's objection with a conditional agreement that moves the sale forward. This technique is effective for handling specific objections directly.

Example:
Scenario: If a prospect is concerned about the price, the salesperson might say, "If I can offer you a discount, are you ready to move forward today?"

7. The Columbo Close

Named after the famous TV detective, the Columbo close involves asking one last question or making one final statement as if an afterthought, often catching the prospect off guard and encouraging them to make a decision.

Example:
Scenario: As the salesperson is wrapping up the conversation, they might say, "Oh, by the way, I almost

forgot to mention, our software comes with a free three-month support package. Does that help you decide?"

Strategies for Overcoming Sales Objections

Active Listening

Active listening involves fully concentrating on what the prospect is saying, understanding their concerns, responding thoughtfully, and remembering the details. This approach helps in accurately identifying the root of the objection and addressing it effectively.

Example:
A prospect expresses concern about the high cost of a new software solution. By actively listening, the salesperson learns that the prospect

is worried about fitting the purchase into their budget. The salesperson can then address this specific concern by offering a payment plan or highlighting cost-saving features of the software.

Empathy and Understanding

Demonstrating empathy and understanding helps build rapport and trust with the prospect. Acknowledging their concerns shows that the salesperson is genuinely interested in finding a solution that works for them.

Example:
If a prospect is hesitant about switching to a new service provider due to past negative experiences, showing empathy and sharing success stories of other clients who

made the switch can help alleviate their concerns.

Clarifying and Validating

Clarification involves asking questions to fully understand the objection, while validation reassures the prospect that their concerns are legitimate. This approach not only addresses the specific objection but also reinforces the salesperson's credibility.

Example:
A prospect expresses uncertainty about the compatibility of a new software with their existing systems. The salesperson can clarify by asking detailed questions about the prospect's current setup and validate their concern by providing case studies or testimonials from other clients with similar systems.

Providing Evidence and Examples

Concrete evidence and examples, such as case studies, testimonials, and demonstrations, can effectively counter objections. Providing proof of past successes and demonstrating the product's benefits can alleviate doubts and build confidence.

Example:
When a prospect questions the ROI of a marketing service, the salesperson can present case studies showing significant ROI achieved by similar businesses. Additionally, offering a demonstration or trial period can provide firsthand experience of the benefits.

Reframing the Objection

Reframing involves turning the objection into a positive aspect or showing a different perspective. This technique helps prospects see the situation in a new light and can diminish their concerns.

Example:
If a prospect objects to the initial cost of a high-quality product, the salesperson can reframe this by emphasizing the long-term savings and superior performance, which ultimately offers better value compared to cheaper alternatives.

Offering Alternatives and Solutions

Flexibility in offering alternatives or customized solutions can address objections effectively. This approach shows that the salesperson is willing to work with the prospect to find a mutually beneficial solution.

Example:
A prospect is concerned about the implementation timeline of a new service. The salesperson can offer alternative solutions, such as phased implementation or additional support, to accommodate the prospect's schedule and alleviate their concerns.

Practical Applications and Real-World Examples

Example 1: Overcoming Price Objections with the Assumptive Close

Scenario: A small business owner is hesitant to invest in a new CRM system due to its high cost.

Approach:

- Active Listening: The salesperson listens to the client's budget concerns and asks questions to understand their financial constraints.
- Providing Evidence: The salesperson presents data showing how the CRM system has helped similar businesses increase revenue and reduce operational costs.
- Assumptive Close: The salesperson asks, "When would you like to start your free trial?"

Outcome: The client, reassured by the evidence and the assumptive close, agrees to start the trial, leading to a successful sale.

Example 2: Addressing Timing Objections with the Urgency Close

Scenario: A potential client is interested in a new project

management tool but feels it's not the right time to switch due to ongoing projects.

Approach:
- Empathy and Understanding: The salesperson acknowledges the client's concern about the timing and expresses understanding.
- Clarifying and Validating: The salesperson asks detailed questions about the client's current projects and timeline.
- Urgency Close: The salesperson emphasizes a limited-time discount for early adopters.

Outcome: The client appreciates the urgency of the offer and agrees to start the implementation process after completing the current projects.

Example 3: Handling Trust Objections with the Feel, Felt, Found Method

Scenario: A client is wary of switching to a new supplier due to a negative experience with a previous supplier.

Approach:
- Empathy and Understanding: The salesperson empathizes with the client's past experiences and acknowledges their hesitation.
- Providing Evidence: The salesperson shares testimonials from satisfied customers and offers a trial period to build trust.
- Feel, Felt, Found Method: "I understand how you feel. Many of our clients initially felt the same way. However, they found that our superior customer service and

support made the transition smooth and beneficial."

Outcome: The client, reassured by the evidence and the Feel, Felt, Found method, decides to give the new supplier a chance, leading to a successful partnership.

Conclusion

Mastering the art of overcoming objections and closing deals is essential for sales success. By employing top sales closing techniques such as the Assumptive Close, Summary Close, Urgency Close, Alternative Choice Close, Question Close, Sharp Angle Close, and Columbo Close, sales professionals can effectively address objections and guide prospects towards making a purchase.

In addition, strategies like active listening, empathy, clarification, validation, providing evidence, reframing objections, and offering alternatives play a crucial role in turning objections into agreements. Real-world examples demonstrate that objections are not barriers but opportunities to engage with prospects, understand their needs, and provide tailored solutions.

By embracing these techniques and strategies, salespeople can enhance their ability to close deals, build long-term customer relationships, and achieve sustained success in their sales careers. Conquering sales objections like a pro is not just about overcoming challenges; it's about transforming them into opportunities for growth

Turning No into Yes: The Ultimate Guide to Closing Sales

In the competitive world of sales, closing deals is both an art and a science. It's a process that requires understanding the customer's needs, addressing their concerns, and ultimately persuading them to say "yes." The ability to effectively close sales distinguishes successful sales professionals from the rest. This report delves into the most effective sales closing techniques, strategies to overcome objections, and real-world examples of how to turn a "no" into a "yes."

Understanding Sales Closes

The Importance of Closing

Closing is the culmination of the sales process. It's the moment when the prospect decides to commit to the purchase. Effective closing techniques can significantly increase conversion rates and drive business growth. Mastering the art of closing involves not only persuasive skills but also empathy, active listening, and strategic thinking.

Types of Sales Closes

1. Assumptive Close: Presumes the sale is a done deal and moves forward with actions that indicate completion.
2. Summary Close: Summarizes the main benefits and features before asking for the sale.
3. Urgency Close: Creates a sense of urgency to prompt immediate action.
4. Alternative Choice Close: Offers the prospect a choice between two positive outcomes.

5. Question Close: Uses questions to guide the prospect toward the decision.
6. Sharp Angle Close: Turns an objection into a conditional agreement.
7. Columbo Close: Uses a final, casual question to nudge the prospect toward closing.

Top Sales Closing Techniques

1. The Assumptive Close

The assumptive close involves acting as if the prospect has already decided to purchase. This technique leverages the power of suggestion and can be highly effective in moving the conversation toward a close.

Example:
Scenario: A salesperson selling a software subscription might say,

"When would you like to schedule your onboarding session?" instead of "Are you ready to buy?"

2. The Summary Close

The summary close involves recapping the key benefits and features of the product or service before asking for the sale. This technique reinforces the value proposition and helps address any lingering doubts.

Example:
Scenario: "To summarize, our software will help streamline your operations, reduce costs, and improve productivity. Shall we go ahead and get you started with a subscription today?"

3. The Urgency Close

Creating a sense of urgency can prompt the prospect to take immediate action. This can be achieved by emphasizing limited-time offers, exclusive deals, or immediate benefits of the product.

Example:
Scenario: "We have a special promotion that ends this week, offering a 20% discount on your first year. Would you like to take advantage of this offer?"

4. The Alternative Choice Close

The alternative choice close presents the prospect with two options, both of which lead to a sale. This technique gives the prospect a sense of control while guiding them towards a decision.

Example:

Scenario: "Would you prefer the standard package or the premium package with additional features?"

5. The Question Close

The question close involves asking questions that lead the prospect to acknowledge the benefits of the product and move closer to a decision. This technique encourages engagement and helps uncover any remaining objections.

Example:
Scenario: "How do you see our product fitting into your current operations and helping you achieve your goals?"

6. The Sharp Angle Close

The sharp angle close involves addressing a prospect's objection with a conditional agreement that moves the sale forward. This technique is effective for handling specific objections directly.

Example:
Scenario: If a prospect is concerned about the price, the salesperson might say, "If I can offer you a discount, are you ready to move forward today?"

7. The Columbo Close

Named after the famous TV detective, the Columbo close involves asking one last question or making one final statement as if an afterthought, often catching the prospect off guard and encouraging them to make a decision.

Example:

Scenario: As the salesperson is wrapping up the conversation, they might say, "Oh, by the way, I almost forgot to mention, our software comes with a free three-month support package. Does that help you decide?"

Strategies for Overcoming Sales Objections

Active Listening

Active listening involves fully concentrating on what the prospect is saying, understanding their concerns, responding thoughtfully, and remembering the details. This approach helps in accurately identifying the root of the objection and addressing it effectively.

Example:

A prospect expresses concern about the high cost of a new software solution. By actively listening, the salesperson learns that the prospect is worried about fitting the purchase into their budget. The salesperson can then address this specific concern by offering a payment plan or highlighting cost-saving features of the software.

Empathy and Understanding

Demonstrating empathy and understanding helps build rapport and trust with the prospect. Acknowledging their concerns shows that the salesperson is genuinely interested in finding a solution that works for them.

Example:
If a prospect is hesitant about switching to a new service provider

due to past negative experiences, showing empathy and sharing success stories of other clients who made the switch can help alleviate their concerns.

Clarifying and Validating

Clarification involves asking questions to fully understand the objection, while validation reassures the prospect that their concerns are legitimate. This approach not only addresses the specific objection but also reinforces the salesperson's credibility.

Example:
A prospect expresses uncertainty about the compatibility of a new software with their existing systems. The salesperson can clarify by asking detailed questions about the prospect's current setup and validate

their concern by providing case studies or testimonials from other clients with similar systems.

Providing Evidence and Examples

Concrete evidence and examples, such as case studies, testimonials, and demonstrations, can effectively counter objections. Providing proof of past successes and demonstrating the product's benefits can alleviate doubts and build confidence.

Example:
When a prospect questions the ROI of a marketing service, the salesperson can present case studies showing significant ROI achieved by similar businesses. Additionally, offering a demonstration or trial period can provide firsthand experience of the benefits.

Reframing the Objection

Reframing involves turning the objection into a positive aspect or showing a different perspective. This technique helps prospects see the situation in a new light and can diminish their concerns.

Example:
If a prospect objects to the initial cost of a high-quality product, the salesperson can reframe this by emphasizing the long-term savings and superior performance, which ultimately offers better value compared to cheaper alternatives.

Offering Alternatives and Solutions

Flexibility in offering alternatives or customized solutions can address objections effectively. This approach shows that the salesperson is willing to work with the prospect to find a mutually beneficial solution.

Example:
A prospect is concerned about the implementation timeline of a new service. The salesperson can offer alternative solutions, such as phased implementation or additional support, to accommodate the prospect's schedule and alleviate their concerns.

Practical Applications and Real-World Examples

Example 1: Overcoming Price Objections with the Assumptive Close

Scenario: A small business owner is hesitant to invest in a new CRM system due to its high cost.

Approach:
- Active Listening: The salesperson listens to the client's budget concerns and asks questions to understand their financial constraints.
- Providing Evidence: The salesperson presents data showing how the CRM system has helped similar businesses increase revenue and reduce operational costs.
- Assumptive Close: The salesperson asks, "When would you like to start your free trial?"

Outcome: The client, reassured by the evidence and the assumptive close, agrees to start the trial, leading to a successful sale.

Example 2: Addressing Timing Objections with the Urgency Close

Scenario: A potential client is interested in a new project management tool but feels it's not the right time to switch due to ongoing projects.

Approach:
- Empathy and Understanding: The salesperson acknowledges the client's concern about the timing and expresses understanding.
- Clarifying and Validating: The salesperson asks detailed questions about the client's current projects and timeline.
- Urgency Close: The salesperson emphasizes a limited-time discount for early adopters.

Outcome: The client appreciates the urgency of the offer and agrees to start the implementation process after completing the current projects.

Example 3: Handling Trust Objections with the Feel, Felt, Found Method

Scenario: A client is wary of switching to a new supplier due to a negative experience with a previous supplier.

Approach:
- Empathy and Understanding: The salesperson empathizes with the client's past experiences and acknowledges their hesitation.
- Providing Evidence: The salesperson shares testimonials from satisfied customers and offers a trial period to build trust.
- Feel, Felt, Found Method: "I understand how you feel. Many of our clients initially felt the same way. However, they found that our superior customer service and

support made the transition smooth and beneficial."

Outcome: The client, reassured by the evidence and the Feel, Felt, Found method, decides to give the new supplier a chance, leading to a successful partnership.

Advanced Techniques for Closing Sales

The Feel, Felt, Found Method

This method involves empathizing with the prospect's feelings, sharing a story of someone who felt the same way, and explaining what they found after using the product.

Example:
Scenario: A prospect is hesitant about the complexity of a new software system.

Approach:
- Feel: "I understand how you feel. Many of our clients initially felt the same way about the complexity."
- Felt: "One of our clients, a mid-sized company, felt overwhelmed at first."
- Found: "But they found that with our comprehensive training and support, they were able to master the software quickly and saw significant improvements in their productivity."

Outcome : The prospect, reassured by the shared experience, is more likely to proceed with the purchase.

The Benjamin Franklin Close

Named after the famous decision-making technique used by Benjamin Franklin, this close involves listing the pros and cons of the product to help the prospect make a logical decision.

 Example:
Scenario: A prospect is on the fence about purchasing a new marketing service.

Approach:
- Pros and Cons List: The salesperson helps the prospect create a list of pros (e.g., increased lead generation, better brand visibility) and cons (e.g., initial cost, learning curve).
- Analyzing the List: The salesperson guides the prospect in weighing the pros against the cons, highlighting the long-term benefits.

Outcome: The prospect sees the value outweighing the drawbacks and decides to move forward with the purchase.

Conclusion

Mastering the art of closing sales and overcoming objections is crucial for sales success. By employing top sales closing techniques such as the Assumptive Close, Summary Close, Urgency Close, Alternative Choice Close, Question Close, Sharp Angle Close, and Columbo Close, sales professionals can effectively address objections and guide prospects towards making a purchase.

In addition, strategies like active listening, empathy, clarification, validation, providing evidence, reframing objections, and offering alternatives play a crucial role in turning objections into agreements. Real-world examples demonstrate that objections are not barriers but opportunities to engage with prospects, understand their needs, and provide tailored solutions.

By embracing these techniques and strategies, salespeople can enhance their ability to close deals, build long-term customer relationships, and achieve sustained success in their sales careers. Turning a "no" into a "yes" is not just about overcoming challenges; it's about transforming them into opportunities for growth and success.

Closing Power: Overcoming Sales Objections for Guaranteed Success

In the world of sales, the journey from generating a lead to closing a deal is often fraught with challenges. One of the most significant hurdles in this journey is overcoming sales objections. These objections, when handled effectively, can turn potential roadblocks into opportunities for building trust and demonstrating value. This report delves into the strategies and techniques for guiding a lead through the sales funnel, overcoming objections, and ensuring a successful close.

Understanding Sales Objections

What Are Sales Objections?

Sales objections are concerns or reasons that prospects give for not moving forward with a purchase. These objections can arise at any stage of the sales process and can pertain to various aspects of the product or service, including price, value, timing, need, and trust. Recognizing and addressing these objections is crucial for maintaining the momentum of the sales conversation.

Common Types of Sales Objections

1. Price Objections: Concerns about the cost of the product or service.
2. Value Objections: Doubts about the benefits or return on investment.
3. Timing Objections: Hesitations related to the timing of the purchase.
4. Need Objections: Uncertainty about whether the product or service meets their needs.
5. Trust Objections: Lack of confidence in the company, product, or salesperson.

The Sales Process: From Lead to Close

1. Lead Generation

The first step in the sales process is generating leads. This involves identifying potential customers who may be interested in your product or service. Effective lead generation strategies include content marketing, social media campaigns, email marketing, networking events, and referrals.

2. Lead Qualification

Once leads are generated, the next step is to qualify them. This involves assessing whether the lead is a good fit for your product or service. Key factors to consider include the lead's budget, authority to make a decision, need for the product, and the timing of their purchase (commonly referred to as BANT: Budget, Authority, Need, Timing).

3. Needs Assessment

During the needs assessment stage, the salesperson engages in a detailed conversation with the lead to understand their specific needs, challenges, and goals. This stage is critical for building rapport and gathering information that will be essential for addressing objections later in the process.

4. Presentation

Based on the needs assessment, the salesperson presents a tailored solution that highlights how the product or service meets the lead's needs and provides value. This presentation should be focused on the benefits and outcomes rather than just the features of the product.

5. Handling Objections

Objections are a natural part of the sales process. The key to overcoming objections is to listen actively, empathize with the lead's concerns, clarify any misunderstandings, and provide evidence or examples to address their doubts.

6. Closing the Sale

The final step in the sales process is closing the sale. This involves using specific closing techniques to guide the lead to make a purchasing decision. Effective closing techniques can help overcome final objections and secure the commitment of the lead.

Effective Strategies for Overcoming Sales Objections

Active Listening

Active listening is the foundation of overcoming sales objections. It involves fully concentrating on what the lead is saying, understanding their concerns, and responding thoughtfully. By demonstrating that you value the lead's perspective, you can build trust and uncover the real reasons behind their objections.

Example:
A prospect is concerned about the cost of a new software solution. By actively listening, the salesperson learns that the prospect is worried about fitting the purchase into their budget. The salesperson can then address this specific concern by offering a payment plan or highlighting cost-saving features of the software.

Empathy and Understanding

Showing empathy and understanding helps build rapport with the lead. Acknowledging their concerns and showing that you genuinely care about finding a solution that works for them can significantly reduce resistance.

Example:
If a prospect is hesitant about switching to a new service provider due to past negative experiences, showing empathy and sharing success stories of other clients who made the switch can help alleviate their concerns.

Clarification and Validation

Clarification involves asking questions to fully understand the objection, while validation reassures the lead that their concerns are legitimate. This approach not only addresses the specific objection but also reinforces the salesperson's credibility.

Example:
A prospect expresses uncertainty about the compatibility of a new software with their existing systems. The salesperson can clarify by asking detailed questions about the prospect's current setup and validate their concern by providing case studies or testimonials from other clients with similar systems.

Providing Evidence and Examples

Concrete evidence and examples, such as case studies, testimonials, and demonstrations, can effectively counter objections. Providing proof of past successes and demonstrating the product's benefits can alleviate doubts and build confidence.

Example:
When a prospect questions the ROI of a marketing service, the salesperson can present case studies showing significant ROI achieved by similar businesses. Additionally, offering a demonstration or trial period can provide firsthand experience of the benefits.

Reframing the Objection

Reframing involves turning the objection into a positive aspect or showing a different perspective. This technique helps prospects see the situation in a new light and can diminish their concerns.

Example:
If a prospect objects to the initial cost of a high-quality product, the salesperson can reframe this by

emphasizing the long-term savings and superior performance, which ultimately offers better value compared to cheaper alternatives.

Offering Alternatives and Solutions

Flexibility in offering alternatives or customized solutions can address objections effectively. This approach shows that the salesperson is willing to work with the lead to find a mutually beneficial solution.

Example:
A prospect is concerned about the implementation timeline of a new service. The salesperson can offer alternative solutions, such as phased implementation or additional support, to accommodate the prospect's schedule and alleviate their concerns.

Top Closing Techniques

1. The Assumptive Close

The assumptive close involves acting as if the prospect has already decided to purchase. This technique leverages the power of suggestion and can be highly effective in moving the conversation toward a close.

Example:
Scenario: A salesperson selling a software subscription might say, "When would you like to schedule your onboarding session?" instead of "Are you ready to buy?"

2. The Summary Close

The summary close involves recapping the key benefits and features of the product or service before asking for the sale. This technique reinforces the value proposition and helps address any lingering doubts.

Example:
Scenario: "To summarize, our software will help streamline your operations, reduce costs, and improve productivity. Shall we go ahead and get you started with a subscription today?"

3. The Urgency Close

Creating a sense of urgency can prompt the prospect to take immediate action. This can be achieved by emphasizing limited-time offers, exclusive deals, or immediate benefits of the product.

Example:
Scenario: "We have a special promotion that ends this week,

offering a 20% discount on your first year. Would you like to take advantage of this offer?"

4. The Alternative Choice Close

The alternative choice close presents the prospect with two options, both of which lead to a sale. This technique gives the prospect a sense of control while guiding them towards a decision.

Example:
Scenario: "Would you prefer the standard package or the premium package with additional features?"

5. The Question Close

The question close involves asking questions that lead the prospect to acknowledge the benefits of the product and move closer to a decision. This technique encourages engagement and helps uncover any remaining objections.

Example:
Scenario: "How do you see our product fitting into your current operations and helping you achieve your goals?"

6. The Sharp Angle Close

The sharp angle close involves addressing a prospect's objection with a conditional agreement that moves the sale forward. This technique is effective for handling specific objections directly.

Example:
Scenario: If a prospect is concerned about the price, the salesperson might say, "If I can offer you a

discount, are you ready to move forward today?"

7. The Columbo Close

Named after the famous TV detective, the Columbo close involves asking one last question or making one final statement as if an afterthought, often catching the prospect off guard and encouraging them to make a decision.

Example:
Scenario: As the salesperson is wrapping up the conversation, they might say, "Oh, by the way, I almost forgot to mention, our software comes with a free three-month support package. Does that help you decide?"

Practical Applications and Real-World Examples

Example 1: Overcoming Price Objections with the Assumptive Close

Scenario: A small business owner is hesitant to invest in a new CRM system due to its high cost.

Approach:
- Active Listening: The salesperson listens to the client's budget concerns and asks questions to understand their financial constraints.
- Providing Evidence: The salesperson presents data showing how the CRM system has helped similar businesses increase revenue and reduce operational costs.
- Assumptive Close: The salesperson asks, "When would you like to start your free trial?"

Outcome: The client, reassured by the evidence and the assumptive close, agrees to start the trial, leading to a successful sale.

Example 2: Addressing Timing Objections with the Urgency Close

Scenario: A potential client is interested in a new project management tool but feels it's not the right time to switch due to ongoing projects.

Approach:
- Empathy and Understanding: The salesperson acknowledges the client's concern about the timing and expresses understanding.
- Clarifying and Validating: The salesperson asks detailed questions about the client's current projects and timeline.

- Urgency Close: The salesperson emphasizes a limited-time discount for early adopters.

Outcome: The client appreciates the urgency of the offer and agrees to start the implementation

Deal Makers: Mastering Objections to Achieve Sales Excellence

Introduction

In the world of sales, closing a deal is the ultimate goal and a true test of a salesperson's skill. However, the path to closing is often fraught with objections from potential clients. These objections can range from concerns about cost to skepticism about product efficacy. Mastering the art of handling objections is crucial for achieving sales excellence. This report delves into strategies for effectively managing objections, emphasizing the transition from addressing concerns to closing the deal successfully.

Understanding Objections

Objections are a natural part of the sales process. They represent the client's concerns and are often seen as hurdles to closing a deal. However, when handled properly, objections can be transformed into opportunities for deeper engagement and stronger client relationships. Common objections include issues related to price, product features, perceived value, and trust. To master objections, it is essential first to understand their root causes.

1. Price Concerns: Clients often express concerns about cost, fearing

that the investment might not yield a sufficient return. Addressing this objection requires demonstrating the value and return on investment (ROI) of the product or service.

2. Product Features and Efficacy: Clients may doubt whether the product meets their needs or performs as advertised. This objection can be countered with detailed explanations, demonstrations, and testimonials.

3. Perceived Value: Sometimes, clients struggle to see the unique value of a product compared to competitors. Differentiation and value proposition are key here.

4. Trust Issues: Trust is fundamental in sales. If a client has doubts about the credibility of the salesperson or the company, building trust through

transparency, reliability, and evidence is essential.

Strategies for Handling Objections

1. Active Listening: The first step in managing objections is to listen actively. This means fully engaging with the client, understanding their concerns without interrupting, and showing empathy. Active listening helps in identifying the underlying issues and demonstrates respect for the client's perspective.

2. Clarification and Validation: After listening, clarify the objection to ensure understanding. Repeat back what the client has said in your own words, and validate their concerns. This builds rapport and shows that their worries are taken seriously.

3. Addressing the Objection: Once the objection is clear, address it directly. Provide relevant information, evidence, and solutions tailored to the specific concern. For example, if the objection is about price, break down the cost versus benefits and provide case studies or testimonials that highlight ROI.

4. Reframing the Objection: Sometimes, objections can be reframed into positive aspects. For instance, if a client is concerned about the complexity of a product, reframe it as a feature-rich solution that offers extensive benefits and long-term value.

5. Empathy and Assurance: Show empathy by acknowledging the client's feelings and concerns. Assure them that their issues are common and manageable. Share

stories of other clients who had similar concerns but benefited greatly after choosing your product or service.

6. Trial Close: Use trial closes to gauge the client's readiness. Phrases like "How does that sound to you?" or "Does this address your concern?" help in assessing whether the client is moving closer to a decision.

Transitioning to the Close

The transition from handling objections to closing the deal is a delicate phase. It requires confidence, timing, and finesse. Here are key strategies for a smooth transition:

1. Summarize and Confirm: After addressing objections, summarize the key points of the discussion. This

helps in reinforcing the value proposition and ensuring that all concerns have been resolved. Confirm the client's agreement on these points.

2. Create a Sense of Urgency: Introduce a sense of urgency to encourage the client to act promptly. This could be through limited-time offers, exclusive discounts, or emphasizing the benefits of early adoption.

3. Assume the Sale: Assuming the sale is a technique where the salesperson proceeds with the next steps as if the client has already decided to buy. This can be effective if done subtly, such as preparing the paperwork or discussing implementation details.

4. Provide Options: Offering choices can make the decision easier for the client. Present different packages or plans, allowing the client to select the one that best suits their needs.

5. Close with Confidence: Confidence is crucial in closing. Make the final ask with confidence and positivity. Use phrases like "Shall we proceed with this option?" or "I can get the contract ready for you."

6. Follow-Up and Reassurance: After the initial close, reassure the client of their decision. Follow up with any additional information or support they might need. This reinforces their choice and helps in building a long-term relationship.

Case Studies

Case Study 1: Price Objection

A software company faced a common objection regarding the high price of their enterprise solution. To address this, the sales team provided a detailed ROI analysis, showcasing how the software reduced operational costs and increased efficiency. They also shared testimonials from existing clients who had experienced significant cost savings. By reframing the price as an investment with substantial returns, they were able to close the deal successfully.

Case Study 2: Trust and Credibility

A new entrant in the healthcare sector struggled with objections related to trust and credibility. The sales team tackled this by highlighting the company's partnerships with reputable organizations, showcasing certifications, and providing trial periods to demonstrate efficacy. Additionally, they encouraged potential clients to speak with existing customers for unbiased feedback. This approach helped build trust and led to increased sales.

Conclusion

Mastering objections is a critical skill for any salesperson aiming for excellence. By understanding the nature of objections and employing effective strategies to address them, sales professionals can turn challenges into opportunities. The transition from handling objections to closing a deal requires a combination of active listening, empathy, and confidence. By summarizing discussions, creating urgency, and assuming the sale, salespeople can smoothly guide clients to a positive decision. Ultimately, the ability to handle objections adeptly not only enhances sales performance but also fosters stronger, more trusting client relationships.

The Art of Persuasion: Closing Sales by Overcoming Objections

Introduction

In the competitive world of sales, mastering the art of persuasion is essential for success. Persuasion involves influencing potential clients' thoughts, feelings, and actions to achieve a desired outcome—in this case, closing a sale. One of the most significant hurdles in this process is overcoming objections. Objections are natural and can arise from various concerns, including price, product features, and trust issues. This report explores persuasive sales tactics specifically aimed at overcoming objections, emphasizing how these strategies can help close sales effectively.

Understanding Objections in Sales

Objections are a form of resistance that clients express when they have concerns or doubts about a product or service. They are not outright rejections but rather an invitation for further dialogue. Common objections include:

1. Price: Clients may feel the product or service is too expensive or not within their budget.
2. Product Features: Doubts about whether the product meets their

specific needs or performs as promised.
3. Value: Clients may question the overall value proposition, wondering if the product is worth the investment.
4. Trust: Concerns about the credibility of the salesperson or the company, including reliability and post-purchase support.

Understanding these objections is the first step in effectively addressing them. Each type of objection requires a tailored approach to overcome it persuasively.

Persuasive Tactics for Overcoming Objections

1. Active Listening and Empathy

Active listening involves fully concentrating, understanding, responding, and then remembering what the client is saying. It shows respect for the client's perspective and helps in identifying the root cause of their objections. Empathy goes hand-in-hand with active listening, as it involves understanding and sharing the feelings of the client.

Example: If a client objects to the price, an empathetic response might be, "I understand that budgeting is a critical factor for your business. Let's explore how this investment can yield significant returns over time."

2. Building Trust and Credibility

Trust is a cornerstone of persuasive sales tactics. Building credibility can be achieved through transparency, showcasing expertise, and providing social proof. Sharing testimonials, case studies, and endorsements from reputable sources can alleviate concerns about trust and reliability.

Example: Providing a potential client with case studies demonstrating how similar businesses have benefited from your product can establish credibility and trust.

3. Reframing Objections

Reframing involves viewing an objection from a different perspective and presenting it as a positive aspect. This technique helps in shifting the client's mindset and highlighting the benefits that outweigh their concerns.

Example: If a client is concerned about the complexity of a product, you could reframe it by emphasizing its advanced features that provide comprehensive solutions, thereby adding more value.

4. Value Proposition and ROI

Effectively communicating the value proposition and return on investment (ROI) is crucial in overcoming objections related to price and value. This involves demonstrating how the product solves the client's problems and delivers measurable benefits.

Example: "While the initial investment is significant, our product reduces operational costs by 30%, leading to a positive ROI within the first year."

5. Trial Offers and Demonstrations

Offering a trial period or product demonstration can mitigate doubts about product efficacy and value.

This hands-on experience allows clients to see the benefits firsthand, reducing perceived risks.

Example: Providing a free trial or a money-back guarantee can persuade clients to try the product without financial risk, making it easier for them to make a purchase decision.

6. Addressing Specific Concerns

Tailoring responses to address specific objections directly and providing evidence to counter those concerns can be highly persuasive. This might include technical specifications, comparison charts, or detailed explanations.

Example: If a client is worried about integration with existing systems, providing a detailed compatibility report and examples of successful integrations can address this concern effectively.

7. Creating a Sense of Urgency

Introducing a sense of urgency can prompt clients to act quickly, overcoming procrastination and indecision. This can be achieved through limited-time offers, exclusive deals, or highlighting the benefits of early adoption.

Example: "This offer is available until the end of the month. By acting now, you can secure a 20% discount and start benefiting from our solution immediately."

Case Studies

Case Study 1: Overcoming Price Objections

A marketing software company frequently encountered objections related to the high cost of their comprehensive solution. To overcome this, the sales team developed a detailed cost-benefit analysis tool that demonstrated the ROI clients could expect. They also shared success stories from clients who had seen significant increases in revenue after using the software. By focusing on the long-term benefits and ROI, they were able to persuade clients to view the cost as a worthwhile investment, leading to a higher conversion rate.

Case Study 2: Addressing Product Complexity

A healthcare technology firm faced objections regarding the complexity of their new patient management system. To counter this, they offered a free, personalized demo and a 30-day trial period. During the demo, they highlighted the system's user-friendly interface and extensive support resources, including training and 24/7 customer service. By allowing potential clients to experience the system firsthand and providing assurances of ongoing support, they successfully overcame the objections and increased sales.

Case Study 3: Building Trust

A financial services company struggled with trust issues due to being relatively new in the market. To build credibility, the sales team emphasized their partnerships with established financial institutions, showcased their compliance with industry regulations, and provided testimonials from satisfied clients. They also offered a free financial assessment to demonstrate their expertise and commitment to client success. These efforts helped build trust and led to increased client acquisition.

Conclusion

Persuasion is a vital skill in sales, particularly when it comes to overcoming objections. By employing tactics such as active listening, empathy, building trust, reframing objections, and clearly communicating value propositions, sales professionals can turn potential barriers into opportunities for engagement and conversion. Offering trials, addressing specific concerns with tailored information, and creating a sense of urgency can further enhance persuasive efforts. Mastering these techniques not only aids in closing more sales but also fosters stronger, more trusting relationships with clients, ultimately leading to long-term success in the competitive world of sales.

Objection Mastery: Proven Strategies to Close Any Sale

Introduction

In the realm of sales, one of the most critical skills is the ability to master objections and turn potential roadblocks into opportunities. This ability, coupled with the effective qualification of sales leads, is what often distinguishes top performers from the rest. Qualifying leads ensures that sales efforts are directed towards prospects who have the highest potential to convert, thereby maximizing efficiency and success rates. This report explores proven strategies for qualifying sales leads and mastering objections to close any sale.

The Significance of Qualifying Sales Leads

Qualifying sales leads is an essential step in the sales process. It involves evaluating potential clients to determine their likelihood of making a purchase. Effective lead qualification helps sales teams prioritize their efforts, focusing on leads that are most likely to convert. This not only saves time but also increases the chances of closing deals successfully. By ensuring that only the most promising leads are pursued, sales professionals can optimize their efforts and resources.

Key Criteria for Qualifying Sales Leads

To qualify sales leads effectively, sales professionals must evaluate prospects based on specific criteria. These criteria help in identifying leads that are worth pursuing and those that may not be a good fit. The BANT framework—Budget, Authority, Need, and Timeline—is widely used for this purpose:

1. Budget: Does the prospect have the financial capacity to purchase the product or service?
2. Authority: Is the prospect the decision-maker, or do they have influence over the decision?
3. Need: Does the prospect have a genuine need for the product or service?
4. Timeline: What is the prospect's timeline for making a decision and implementing the solution?

By assessing leads based on these criteria, sales professionals can ensure that they are targeting the right prospects and allocating their resources effectively.

Strategies for Qualifying Sales Leads

1. Research and Pre-Qualification

Before engaging with a potential lead, conducting thorough research is crucial. This involves gathering information about the prospect's industry, company size, market position, and recent developments. Pre-qualification can be done through online research, social media, and company websites. This background information helps in tailoring the sales approach and identifying whether the prospect meets the BANT criteria.

Example: If a salesperson is targeting a technology company, they might research the company's latest product launches, financial health, and key decision-makers. This information can help in crafting a personalized pitch and understanding whether the company has the budget and need for the salesperson's product.

2. Effective Communication and Discovery Calls

Discovery calls are an essential part of the lead qualification process. During these calls, sales professionals should ask open-ended questions to gather detailed information about the prospect's needs, challenges, and decision-making process. Effective communication is key to building rapport and trust, which are crucial for extracting honest and valuable insights.

Example: Questions such as "What challenges are you currently facing in your operations?" and "Can you walk me through your decision-making process?" help in understanding the prospect's pain points and the internal dynamics of their organization.

3. Utilizing Sales Automation Tools

Sales automation tools can streamline the lead qualification process. These tools can help in tracking prospect interactions, scoring leads based on their engagement, and automating follow-up activities. By leveraging technology, sales teams can ensure that no potential lead falls through the cracks and that high-priority leads are addressed promptly.

Example: CRM systems like Salesforce or HubSpot can track email opens, link clicks, and website visits, providing valuable insights into a prospect's level of interest and engagement. This information can be used to prioritize leads and tailor follow-up actions.

4. Implementing Lead Scoring Models

Lead scoring involves assigning numerical values to various actions taken by prospects, such as downloading a whitepaper, attending a webinar, or requesting a demo. This helps in quantifying the level of interest and engagement, making it easier to prioritize leads that are more likely to convert.

Example: A lead scoring model might assign higher points to actions that indicate a strong buying intent, such as requesting a product demo or signing up for a free trial. Leads with higher scores can then be prioritized for follow-up.

5. Regularly Reviewing and Updating Lead Qualification Criteria

The business environment is dynamic, and lead qualification criteria should reflect current market conditions and business priorities. Regularly reviewing and updating these criteria ensures that sales teams are always focusing on the most relevant and high-potential leads.

Example: A company may update its qualification criteria to focus more on specific industries that have shown increased demand for their product due to recent market trends. This helps in aligning sales efforts with current business goals.

Mastering Objections to Close Sales

Once leads are qualified, the next step is to master objections that may arise during the sales process. Objections are a natural part of sales and often provide opportunities to address concerns and build stronger relationships with prospects. Here are proven strategies to master objections:

1. Active Listening and Empathy

Active listening involves fully concentrating, understanding, responding, and remembering what the prospect is saying. Empathy goes hand-in-hand with active listening, as it involves understanding and sharing the prospect's feelings. These skills are crucial for building trust and rapport, which are essential for overcoming objections.

Example: If a prospect expresses concern about the cost of a product, an empathetic response might be, "I understand that budget is a significant consideration. Let's explore how our product can provide value and deliver a strong return on investment."

2. Reframing Objections

Reframing involves viewing an objection from a different perspective and presenting it as a positive aspect. This technique helps in shifting the prospect's mindset and highlighting the benefits that outweigh their concerns.

Example: If a prospect is concerned about the complexity of a product, a salesperson might reframe it by emphasizing its advanced features and how they provide comprehensive solutions, ultimately adding more value.

3. Providing Social Proof and Evidence

Social proof, such as testimonials, case studies, and endorsements, can be highly persuasive in overcoming objections. Providing evidence that other clients have successfully used the product and achieved positive results helps in building credibility and trust.

Example: Sharing a case study of a similar company that faced the same challenges but saw significant improvements after using the product can help in addressing the prospect's concerns and building confidence in the solution.

4. Clarifying Misconceptions

Sometimes objections arise from misunderstandings or misconceptions about the product. Clarifying these misconceptions by providing accurate and detailed information can help in alleviating concerns.

Example: If a prospect believes that the product lacks certain features, the salesperson can provide detailed product specifications and demonstrate how the product meets all their requirements.

5. Highlighting the Value Proposition and ROI

Effectively communicating the value proposition and return on investment (ROI) is crucial in overcoming objections related to price and value. This involves demonstrating how the product solves the prospect's problems and delivers measurable benefits.

Example: "While the initial investment is significant, our product reduces operational costs by 30%, leading to a positive ROI within the first year."

6. Using the 'Feel, Felt, Found' Technique

The 'Feel, Felt, Found' technique is a classic objection-handling method. It involves acknowledging the prospect's feelings, sharing how others have felt the same way, and explaining what they found after using the product.

Example: "I understand how you feel about the initial cost. Many of our clients felt the same way at first, but they found that the cost savings and efficiency gains they experienced more than justified the investment."

Case Studies

Case Study 1: Qualifying and Overcoming Budget Objections

A software company faced frequent objections related to the high cost of their enterprise solution. To qualify leads more effectively, they implemented a lead scoring model that prioritized prospects with higher budget capacities. During the sales process, they addressed budget objections by providing detailed ROI analyses and sharing success stories from existing clients. By demonstrating the long-term value and cost savings, they successfully converted high-priority leads into customers.

Case Study 2: Addressing Product Complexity Concerns

A healthcare technology firm often encountered objections regarding the complexity of their new patient management system. They qualified leads by focusing on larger healthcare providers with more advanced technological capabilities. During the sales process, they offered personalized demos and free trial periods, highlighting the system's user-friendly interface and extensive support resources. This approach helped in alleviating concerns about complexity and led to increased sales.

Case Study 3: Building Trust in a New Market

A financial services company struggled with trust issues due to being relatively new in the market. They qualified leads by targeting small to medium-sized businesses that were open to innovative solutions. To build trust, they emphasized their partnerships with established financial institutions, showcased their compliance with industry regulations, and provided testimonials from satisfied clients. Offering a free financial assessment further demonstrated their expertise and commitment to client success, resulting in higher client acquisition rates.

Conclusion

Mastering objections and qualifying sales leads are fundamental skills for achieving sales excellence. By utilizing effective qualification criteria such as the BANT framework and employing strategies like thorough research, discovery calls, sales automation, lead scoring, and regular updates to qualification criteria, sales professionals can focus their efforts on the most promising prospects. Additionally, mastering objections through active listening, empathy, reframing, providing social proof, clarifying misconceptions, highlighting the value proposition, and using techniques like 'Feel, Felt, Found' can turn potential roadblocks into opportunities for closing sales. These strategies not only increase the likelihood of closing deals but also foster stronger, more trusting relationships with clients, ultimately leading to long-term success in the competitive world of sales.

Yes, You Can! Overcoming Objections and Closing Deals

Introduction

In the dynamic world of sales, closing deals quickly and efficiently is a paramount objective. The ability to handle objections effectively is a critical component of this process. Sales objections can arise at any stage, from initial contact to final negotiations, and overcoming them can significantly speed up the sales cycle. This report explores strategies for addressing objections and closing sales contracts more rapidly, enabling sales professionals to achieve their targets and enhance their performance.

Understanding Sales Objections

Sales objections are expressions of concern or hesitation from potential clients. These objections can stem from various factors, including price, product features, perceived value, and trust. Understanding the nature of these objections is the first step towards addressing them effectively. Common objections include:

1. Price: The product or service is perceived as too expensive.
2. Product Features: Doubts about whether the product meets specific needs or performs as advertised.

3. Value: Uncertainty about the overall value proposition and return on investment.

4. Trust: Concerns about the credibility and reliability of the salesperson or company.

By understanding these common objections, sales professionals can prepare strategies to address and overcome them.

Strategies for Overcoming Objections

1. Active Listening and Empathy

Active listening involves fully concentrating on what the prospect is saying, understanding their concerns, and responding thoughtfully. Empathy, the ability to understand and share the feelings of another, is crucial in building rapport and trust. When prospects feel heard and understood, they are more likely to be receptive to the salesperson's solutions.

Example: If a prospect objects to the price, an empathetic response might be, "I understand that budgeting is a significant concern. Let's discuss how our product can provide value and potentially save costs in the long run."

2. Reframing Objections

Reframing involves turning an objection into a positive aspect. This technique shifts the prospect's perspective and highlights the benefits that outweigh their concerns. By reframing objections, sales professionals can help prospects see the value in their offering.

Example: If a prospect is concerned about the complexity of a product, a salesperson might reframe it by emphasizing the advanced features that provide comprehensive solutions and long-term benefits.

3. Providing Social Proof

Social proof, such as testimonials, case studies, and endorsements, can be highly persuasive. Demonstrating that other clients have successfully used the product and achieved positive results helps build credibility and trust. This approach can alleviate concerns and encourage prospects to move forward.

Example: Sharing a case study of a similar company that faced the same challenges but saw significant improvements after using the product can help address the prospect's concerns and build confidence in the solution.

4. Clarifying Misconceptions

Sometimes, objections arise from misunderstandings or misconceptions about the product. Providing accurate and detailed information can help clarify these misconceptions and alleviate concerns. This approach requires a deep understanding of the product and the ability to communicate its features and benefits effectively.

Example: If a prospect believes that the product lacks certain features, the salesperson can provide detailed product specifications and demonstrate how the product meets all their requirements.

5. Highlighting the Value Proposition and ROI

Communicating the value proposition and return on investment (ROI) is crucial in overcoming objections related to price and value. This involves demonstrating how the product solves the prospect's problems and delivers measurable benefits. By focusing on the long-term value and cost savings, sales professionals can persuade prospects to view the purchase as a worthwhile investment.

Example: "While the initial investment is significant, our product reduces operational costs by 30%, leading to a positive ROI within the first year."

6. Using the 'Feel, Felt, Found' Technique

The 'Feel, Felt, Found' technique is a classic objection-handling method. It involves acknowledging the prospect's feelings, sharing how others have felt the same way, and explaining what they found after using the product. This approach helps in building empathy and demonstrating that the objection is common and manageable.

Example: "I understand how you feel about the initial cost. Many of our clients felt the same way at first, but they found that the cost savings and efficiency gains they experienced more than justified the investment."

Strategies for Closing Sales Contracts Quicker

1. Creating a Sense of Urgency

Creating a sense of urgency can prompt prospects to act quickly, overcoming procrastination and indecision. This can be achieved through limited-time offers, exclusive deals, or highlighting the benefits of early adoption. By emphasizing the time-sensitive nature of the offer, sales professionals can encourage prospects to make a decision sooner.

Example: "This offer is available until the end of the month. By acting now, you can secure a 20% discount and start benefiting from our solution immediately."

2. Simplifying the Sales Process

A complex and cumbersome sales process can slow down decision-making. Simplifying the process by providing clear and concise information, minimizing paperwork, and offering streamlined purchasing options can help speed up the closing process. Ensuring that the steps to purchase are straightforward and easy to follow can reduce friction and encourage quicker decisions.

Example: Providing an easy-to-understand proposal with a straightforward pricing structure and a simple contract can make it easier for the prospect to say yes.

3. Offering Flexible Payment Terms

Flexible payment terms can make a significant difference in closing sales contracts quicker. By offering options such as installment plans, deferred payments, or discounts for early payment, sales professionals can address budget concerns and make the purchase more accessible to prospects.

Example: "We understand that budget planning is crucial. We can offer you an installment plan that spreads the cost over six months, making it easier to fit within your budget."

4. Leveraging Technology

Technology can play a crucial role in accelerating the sales process. Tools such as electronic signatures, online payment systems, and automated follow-up emails can streamline the closing process and reduce delays. By leveraging technology, sales professionals can ensure that administrative tasks do not hold up the deal.

Example: Using an electronic signature platform allows prospects to sign contracts quickly and easily, eliminating the need for printing, scanning, and mailing documents.

5. Proactive Follow-Up

Proactive follow-up is essential for keeping the momentum going and addressing any lingering concerns. Regular communication, prompt responses to inquiries, and consistent updates can help in maintaining the prospect's interest and moving the deal forward. By staying engaged and showing commitment, sales professionals can build trust and encourage quicker decision-making.

Example: Following up with a phone call or email shortly after the initial meeting to address any questions and provide additional information can demonstrate attentiveness and dedication to the prospect's needs.

Case Studies

Case Study 1: Overcoming Price Objections

A software company frequently encountered objections related to the high cost of their enterprise solution. To address this, the sales team provided detailed ROI analyses and shared success stories from existing clients who had seen significant cost savings and productivity improvements. By focusing on the long-term benefits and demonstrating the value of the investment, they were able to overcome price objections and close deals more quickly.

Case Study 2: Addressing Product Complexity Concerns

A healthcare technology firm faced objections regarding the complexity of their new patient management system. They offered personalized demos and free trial periods to address these concerns, highlighting the system's user-friendly interface and extensive support resources. By allowing potential clients to experience the system firsthand and providing assurances of ongoing support, they successfully alleviated concerns about complexity and accelerated the closing process.

Case Study 3: Building Trust in a New Market

A financial services company struggled with trust issues due to being relatively new in the market.

To build credibility, the sales team emphasized their partnerships with established financial institutions, showcased their compliance with industry regulations, and provided testimonials from satisfied clients. Additionally, they offered a free financial assessment to demonstrate their expertise and commitment to client success. These efforts helped build trust and led to quicker client acquisition.

Conclusion

Closing sales contracts quickly and efficiently is a critical goal for sales professionals. By mastering objections and implementing strategies such as active listening, empathy, reframing objections, providing social proof, clarifying misconceptions, highlighting value propositions, and using the 'Feel,

Felt, Found' technique, sales professionals can overcome objections effectively. Additionally, creating a sense of urgency, simplifying the sales process, offering flexible payment terms, leveraging technology, and proactive follow-up can significantly speed up the closing process. These strategies not only enhance the likelihood of closing deals but also foster stronger, more trusting relationships with clients, ultimately leading to long-term success in the competitive world of sales. Yes, you can overcome objections and close deals—quickly and confidently.

www.ingramcontent.com/pod-product-compliance
Lightning Source LLC
Chambersburg PA
CBHW052258220526
45471CB00001B/397